In Conversation with Myself

J.K. Wilson

BookLeaf
Publishing

India | USA | UK

Presentation by *BookLeaf Publishing*

Web: www.bookleafpub.com

E-mail: info@bookleafpub.com

ISBN: 9789358735147

First edition 2023

For everyone out there who doesn't have a voice—you are heard.

ACKNOWLEDGEMENTS

~ "How to Measure Time" previously published in Garfield Lake Review 2019

~ A special thank you to my mother for never giving up on me, no matter how far fetched my dream may have seemed, and to my father for inspiring me to become a writer in the first place.

~ To the love of my life: thank you for showing me that there is still some good left in this world. Thank you for showing me how to be patient and love every unwanted part of my mind that can drive us crazy at times. Thank you for not leaving my side when I needed you the most and for always backing up my choices.

In Conversation with Myself

Table of Contents

In Conversation with Myself — I

Suppose I was to begin by saying I had fallen in love
with the reverse situation life is supposed to be
as if to say the sky could be momentarily green
clouds molded from blades of grass
how my feet would make home in marshmallow fluff—
would I float? Or perhaps trudge along
like wading in the shallows
of saltwater oceans on the West Coast
defy gravity—like Shel Silverstein could I possibly Fall
Up? Would it be falling?
or perhaps more like lucid dancing through the air?

Suppose I was to say that my family tree
was all wrong—growing down heavy with generations
and, in fact, I was the one not obscure,
but poetically purposed—set microcosmically
at will in a universe entirely my own
where gender was fluid and race didn't matter
built on the foundation of love and essence connection

Suppose I told you I was not wrong,
not broken, not backwards,
merely being viewed upside   down
would you love me in spite of this
instead of trying to flip me around?

A Lesson in Self-love

Cold food is an acquired taste
offered as a reminder that my body
loves to cook—eating not so much
I am filled by the aroma of possibility
forced for the rest of the day to stare
endlessly at a creation that could
benefit me, if only I could find
energy to reach out and consume
what remains flat in front of me
while I lay in bed
somehow knowing that it's hard to
care for a person who I don't
really want to care for
because the world has deemed me
to be a waste of time
the rotation around the sun
will happen regardless, multiple times
before I find the capability to force down
the food that once screamed at me
to be loved, left in the corner, gone cold
the delicious possibility having left
days ago, feeling ignored

World Peace

I am angry at the world
for stripping me bare of everything,
anything making me me.
It's like, am I even allowed to wish
for world peace, if I am this angry?
I hate crying in public
because I grew up to believe
that crying made you weak.
I learned this from my mom,
of course, she never said that.
She did, however, say once
that she wanted a martini
when she broke her toe—
vacuuming, of all things.
Me, being ten, and obedient,
as obedient as a ten-year-old could be
ran to the kitchen, and back
to the hallway, where I cried
because I didn't know how to
make a martini. My mom didn't drink
in front of her kids,
my mom did not cry in front of her kids.
That day was how I learned to be strong — stoic,
from the strongest woman I know.
I did see my mom cry once,
the day she dropped me off in another province
for university. Now, I think it was more terrifying
to see her cry, than to leave
my entire family fourteen hours behind.

II.

When I was fourteen years old,
I watched one hundred and fifty-six
hours on YouTube to learn
how to be pretty, but I was too fat to be pretty,
like, sorry my metabolic rate
isn't the same as it was when I was four.
I always felt the need to apologize
for taking up more room than a size two.
I think about it now—
those YouTube hours sure paid off,
all one hundred and fifty-six of them
learning how to create elaborate hairstyles.
Good thing I got dreads, right, roll out of bed
to put those one hundred and fifty-six
hours of my time to use.

III.

When I was sixteen I was told
by the boy I loved more than cherry pie
(which was a big deal,
considering it was my favourite at the time)
that I would in fact be good enough
to sleep with because
it would be like having sex on a cloud,
but sadly, I wouldn't make the cut
for being seen with him in public
because clouds are meant for dreams
to be kept far away—
because they take up too much space out in public.
In case you didn't catch that, it was because I was fat.
I never wanted to have sex with him,

or maybe I did. Maybe some naive
part of me thought that if I gave this
boy a gift I could never get back,
he would fall madly in love with me too.
A year later, when it finally happened, sex, it was not
romantic.
In fact, it kind of meant nothing other than the fact that
this boy
didn't still want to be a virgin by twenty.
This boy never loved me.
I believe he went to Europe for a while;
I like to imagine, to get away from me,
but that would probably be giving me too much credit.

IV.

I used to recite, sticks and stones
may break my bones, but words
will never hurt me.
Only, the words did hurt me.
The words invaded my body
and chipped away at my identity
bit by bit—
taking on an identity of their own,
until my body
my beautiful curvaceous body
was no longer my body,
merely an object on display for people
to poke and prod at as if they owned me.
Their words owned me because
I became a reflection of what they said I was.

V.

See, I live in an over-sexualized society where
my opinion matters
little, if at all. My work, much like my body
is constantly on display, being graded by the same society
that made me hate every bone inside of me.
So, if my body is no longer my body,
is my work even considered my work?
I was told finally in university that the page was
meant to be a safe place,
so was my body; look at what society did to that.
Just because
I cannot fit into a size two means that I am no longer safe?
How does that work? It doesn't—

I was told that I was angry because my work finally started
to scratch at the surface of what I needed to say.
Mostly I used to write about leaves on the trees and
the wonders
of the night sky. I was told that anything could be poetry.
I never wrote about things like rape,
or words like silence—
I didn't write about controversial issues
because I was so fucking terrified
of the eyes of society, the ones that lurked in the dark
trying to catch me off guard so they could attack my core,
my body, that wasn't really mine.

So, I guess I'm angry.
I was told that it wasn't attractive
when a woman was angry, like one of those
crazy feminists
screaming at men, which is ironic because
apparently, I'm a little angry, and I'm also a feminist,
but I'm not like an angry feminist though,

because then I wouldn't be pretty.
Aren't I pretty?
Dressed up and still over-sexualized
the way you taught me to be; a good girl always abides,
and is always quiet, isn't that right?
My work in turn became
a direct reflection of the stranger
you made me. Yet, I guess, somehow,
despite the fact that I'm angry,
I do still want world peace.
I want to live in a world where words build
people up and don't take control
of their physical sense of being.
I want to wake up proud every single day, feeling safe
because I have claim to my body and to my work,
every single word of it.

First Impression

I don't get invited out often because
I am usually around only for business
which requires shoes
and when that is over, my feet are
instantly bare, which is strange
and that makes people uncomfortable

I have troubles sitting still
when in public because
it is as if the city has swallowed me
and that can be quite overwhelming

Every pair of eyes on me seem
to know about the staph infection
I got when I was eleven from
overplucking my right eyebrow and
half my face went numb in the hotel

So, now I draw on my eyebrows to
hide the scar of missing hair because
I am too proud of the left
to pluck it to match

This makes every first impression
of me a lie—I am nothing more than a fraud

I'm Fine

I'm not ok even though I phone you
and say that I am.
I wasn't well when I left home.
I shouldn't have gone,
but I would have been worse if I stayed.
I wish I could have said at fourteen
what I am finally able to now.
Mom, I don't think I'm ok.

Each day I'm doing the best that I can to navigate
my way through this world that makes no sense at all.
I suffer the anguish of not knowing
why every bone in my body hurts.

I hide for days at a time, through stories
where I am a pirate — Captain Jack Sparrow sometimes.
Remember how I used to play that at school when I was
eight?
Well, now I am a pirate sailing through the ocean of my
mind,
attempting (feebly, I might add) to not be swallowed
whole by waves that are my emotions, because underwater
nobody can hear me scream and nobody will find me
drowning
because on the outside I'm not really drowning.
On the outside I am on the island that only I can find,
if I've been there before and I've been there so many times,
where I drown my sorrows in alcohol, wake the
next morning in accusatory
tone, asking why is the rum always gone?
I drink and drink and drink until I think I might die,

dehydration consuming every square inch of flesh
covering my aching bones. I drink until it's time to leave
and somehow, I know I can because, "I'm Captain Jack
Sparrow."
Back to the ocean inside, only this time I'm really not sure
I'll survive.
Mom, I'm lost inside, too far out for you to find.
I've been gone for months.

Just when I think I won't survive this battle,
I am in Nazi Germany. I went away to fight
a war that only I can win.
I am the best fighter in the world
Mom, you should know that. I've been face to face with
death
so many times, since eleven years old.
I have fought this battle over and over again in my mind,
my body showing physical battle scars each time I go on
the mission,
it's suicide—
I know, but somehow, I come out on the other side, very
much alive
It's not in my head where I hide anymore, but in the
classroom, the library,
at a job I literally despise every last thing about, because
where can I possibly hide when I am trying to hide
from the horrible images inside my mind?

Mom, sometimes I think that I'm dying,
that I'm too far out in the ocean of my mind to be kept in
reality.
I'm not afraid to be locked away,
I'm afraid to be left alone inside my head.
I want to call and talk sometimes, but I don't want the
conversation to
change, as if you don't believe that I can live on my own,

but also, I don't want to feel like we purposely dance
around me either
like doing the bunny hop (I always loved that)
just to avoid the subject, because sometimes I'm fine,
I swear, and I live in the real world
with real people who cause me real pain.
Mom, there is so much pain all the time.
I don't know how to say it sometimes—
Like when I relapsed on drugs last year,
after nearly four years clean Mom, I was dying. I was
waiting to die
and I didn't tell you how bad it got because I didn't want
you to worry.
Mom, remember how scared I was when I phoned
you about the meeting with my professor,
because she found out before you did?
Remember how I thought she hated me and wouldn't
forgive me?
Mom, it was me who hated me,
and me who still doesn't forgive myself for being that
selfish a person.
Some days I hate myself so much and the monster
that lives as an overbearing roommate in need of eviction.
I didn't think I would live past seventeen, but here I am at
twenty-three
with literally no idea what I'm doing. I didn't know I was
this angry
and that it's ok to not be ok sometimes. I know you want to
help,
but I'm sorry, Mom, you can't. I have to go back to the
ocean
of my mind that I have sailed so many times. I have to tame
the waters and navigate my way home. I might not be ok
every moment
of every single day, but I am trying my hardest to figure out
how.

I know you worry Mom, but trust me when I say
that even though I'm not ok right now, I know that
someday
I will be, and for right now I am exactly where I am
supposed to be.
I am on an island in the middle of the ocean of my mind,
and I am learning how to swim so that I am able to survive.
Mom, I think that if you trust me, someday I will be ok.

In Conversation with Myself — II

You, my dear, are a crimson rose snipped
from the branch you bloomed
and trimmed of all thistles and thorns
they smoothed you out,
displayed you on a table
then forgot you in that vase
filled with stale, murky water
set to die in the corner
Now your silky crimson petals
turn black—fall on the floor
swept up and thrown in the trash
new flowers displayed in your place

Reality Check

Do you want to know what it's like to do meth,
to be so high you forget your own name?

Do you want to know what it's like to blink
and have four hours gone, to have all perception of
time distorted?

To have your legs shake against your will,
your palms sticky with slime thicker than sweat,
and your body in shock and feels freezing cold but you're
hot,
where your heart beats out of sync, first way too fast,
and then slower and slower until not at all,
and then way too fast again to catch back up?

Your body convulses—
contorts until you vomit
too desperately to rid your body
of this unknown substance.

This is a Vine, a single six-second loop
captured in the time it takes for
the powdered lines caressing the mirror
to pass from your burning, bleeding chapped nose
into your bloodstream.

Your pupils dilate; teeth grind.
In this moment you are infinite,
you are the helium inside the rubber balloon
causing it to float from the floor.
You possess the power you wish you had when sober;
Every insecurity is put on hold.

Then you blink; it's gone—
Time to repeat.

You swish your hair over your shoulder,
roll up the five dollar bill,
move the razor blade to the side
pause for a moment and stare at the mirror.
You are high.
View this face— remember this moment
Charcoal shadow and liner chunks
sunken into sleepless skin,
dirty eyes, cheeks pale in contrast.
You plug one side of your nose and inhale deeply
with the other.
It hits you again and the image of dirt,
the feeling of utter disgust flits away—
a purple butterfly not meant to stay.
Images sharpen sight increases
as if watching your life on high definition television
everything too magnified, too crisp to watch.
Suddenly everything
that didn't make sense is perfectly clear,
nothing else in the world matters.
You are lost in this moment
content to be both here and nowhere simultaneously.

Then you repeat—
Repeat, repeat, and repeat.

Now it's gone — Everything is gone.
Three hundred dollars, almost a month's rent — gone.
Another day — gone.
All the power you had,
that you were Iron Man in a world of Tony Starks — gone.

You become invaded by pure green rage

racing through your blood.
More, you need more—
The sharp anguish builds in your chest.
You punch the wall. Knuckles bruised and mangled, more.
The pain does not faze you. More.
You offer to suck dick—
your roommate's, no, best friend's boyfriend's dick.
You have crossed the line. Do you care? No.
More. There is no more.
Tears, thick black sludge released,
an emotional landslide, invades.
Dithering mindless spasms and chapped lips.

Nothing makes sense, vision fades—
Where are your glasses?
You forgot for a moment that you actually needed them.
The snake tattoo inked upon your arm—
The Dark Mark, setting you apart from innocence
in its very name
The Dark Mark,
slithers down towards veins, fangs jumping towards
your wrist and bite into flesh.
It hisses at you as it takes skin in its mouth.
Your best friend screams at you.
What are you doing?
Focus, funny, now you must consciously think to focus,
move your eyes downward.
Blood trickles down, showers over the snake.
This was not you,
but the razor blade in your left hand would beg to differ.

Then a face, her face, Rebecca's face,
a girl not even sixteen, dead and mangled
almost unrecognizable enters your brain.
Guilt washes through you, dirty murky
viscous disgust replaces the blood.

Veins are black protruding lesions from your arms.
She cries to you, thin wispy hollow cries from beyond.
Palms cover your ears, fingers grasp at greasy strands,
filthy, unwashed, sweat-covered hair.

Uninvited guests never leave when you want them to.
You know that meth killed her seven years ago,
you know how she looked as she pulled away from you,
thin, pale, all First Nations glow gone from skin,
rough and scabbed, brittle broken hair,
eyes always looking past you, but where?
You watched your childhood friend leave,
heard of her death from an outside source,
remember the way you fell to your knees
and bawled in the school cafeteria,
half-eaten apple dropped from your hand
and rolled on the carpet.

You blink, silence—
Alone in a room, a familiar room.
Lime walls plastered with Jonas Brothers at every angle,
pink psychedelic floral comforter tops a bed.
A body, more like a puppet really,
limp and soft, non-human crumpled on the floor.
The air smells foul, stale, makes you gag.
Vomit soaks the rose carpet.
A small sob escapes you.
Just eighteen—a child still when you almost died
for the first time,
woken up days later by some mysterious source still
unknown to you.
Sworn to start again and live life clean you rise,
shaking legs lift this sad, sickly,
boney, scabbed portrayal of you off the carpet
and onto the bed where you curl into the fetal
position and sob.

Pain in your chest—just a hallucination.

Eyes open, knees hugged to chest,
jeans ripped down the front, your face is hot,
back rested upon the couch, on the floor you rock
back and forth,
Where did you go?
Blood splashes on ripped grey skull shirt
filled with holes now turning brown,
crusty remnants of psychosis cover arms and face.
Where did you go?
Where are you now?
Who are you?
Is anything you see before you real?
You scream, your throat raw,
you taste blood,
feel the desperation, confusion,
rise from your diaphragm.
You scream—you scream until the blackness,
the heavy weight of night washes over you.

You blink. Sun rises, then sinks, then rises again.
Still you have not slept.
Your body is stiff, knees tucked to chest,
the rocking continues.
What day is it?
How much time has passed?
Three, no, four days gone?
Was it not just Sunday?
Can't go to school, filled with shame,
you hide behind overly dramatic black eyes,
vague cliché images and sadly average marks
because you are too terrified to try.

Time passes, but nothing changes.
The only difference is now the days suck,

seem to drudge on and never quite end.
You cannot sleep at night in fear of seeing her face again—
judgment of what you've become.
Poor Rebecca.
Now you are depressed as shit, but hey,
at least you are seven weeks clean,
that's like what, forty-nine days?
Still, you don't want to go to class, like ever,
most days can't even come
up with the energy to leave your fucking bed.

Do you really want to know what it's like to do meth?
It's like a boulder plummeting from a cliff
down upon your head, crushing every bone in your body.
It's watching yourself in the third person
destroy what little good you have left,
lying constantly to those who used to love and trust you,
and then getting so mixed up in which lie you told who and
when.
It's watching those you love leave.
It's the most selfish thing you can do.
It's shredding what little dignity you had left just
for one more line.
The worst part is, it's knowing every second
of every single fucking day
that you would do it again in a heartbeat

Sensory Perception Disorder

I.

It's like a shirt,
you know those super stretchy
one size fits all, fat roll hiding tank tops
that pop your boobs out just right,
but make you feel like
the seams may burst if you breathe
from anywhere other than
the shattered nasal cavities
that are blocked by infections
that spread to your ears
which causes cochlear fluid imbalances

II.

and the room is spinning and your chest hurts
and even though you can't breathe at all
or hear, the static white noise
and blurred screaming of children
cause you to hyperventilate
air that isn't there
and when the cars fly and faces are smashed
the eyes are spillways flooded level by level
and your throat scratched raw
screaming out for somebody to listen
but it's as if everybody
is staring right through you
like you are a holographic projection
of a television character from the 1950s—
a dated reference from before
even your own time

III.

and your heart is the band that plays
where the drummer
is off tempo slightly, not even a whole beat
and tries too hard to catch up
but it's so loud and the one constant
you're able to focus on
nicotine sticks are the only fix
but the eyes, there are so many eyes
they're all fixated on you
watching you from ceiling tiles
and smudged fingerprints on the windows
that should have been cleaned months ago
but somehow, we're forgotten
why are the damn windows always forgotten?

IV.

hands are fat balloons and feet are too
swollen just before the popping point
they are red and hot and begin to sweat
but they feel so cold always cold
crying and perspiring and clammy
and burning and nails are brittle
and want to claw at a face
that's unrecognized
but they would shatter beneath the skin
and be craterous incisions
poisoning the blood that pumps too fast
through vessels that are too restricted

V.

The paint on the walls is
static feedback on the television
when the input is wrong
why is the input always wrong?
And you want to look away
but your eyes can't seem to stop staring
as it sucks you inside
even though mom told you you'd go blind
but it seems so bright and soft
inviting you to the void
that happy nothingness you so badly crave
where there are so many imperfections
they all meld together
becoming nothing—
how badly you want to be
Nothing
like the static that is the paint
in the walls when you stare too long

Puff of Happiness

I wore you like the orb of smoke
          rimming the right sleeve of my cardigan
                    finding your way to the skin
          hovering just above my hand
as if your essence could dissipate
          if scrubbed hard enough
               washed from my life in a moment,
          but I smoked a lot of cigarettes
so, I knew you would be back—
          if not forever,
at least for a little while

Sex is a Disease

Mom asks me if I'm gay, as if
waiting for me to come out because
I told her I was not opposed to the idea
of loving a woman—because
love is love and that is beautiful

The thing with sexuality
is that it can be quite extensive,
the only problem is, it doesn't
include the concept terrified
which pretty much sums up my life

See, sex is a disease for me—
causes my skin to boil under the surface
blisters emerge, filled with anxiety and stress
of the thought of you, the first man's hands
who used me for your advantage

I lay awake at night, trace my lips
with my fingers, imagining the grooves
of your lips to fit perfectly in mine
dry and chapped—hard pressed
our flesh forever locked

I used to think I would lose my virginity
in a pink hued room at sunset
to the song Take my Breath Away
I saw this on Top Gun when I was eleven
because everything we see in the movies is real

Now, when I say Take my Breath Away
I didn't mean my ability to breathe
because you covered my face
with a pillow to stop me from screaming
when I didn't actually want to be touched

See, sex is a cancer spreading through my bones
tumors holding me hostage in a bed
I can't rise from—
even though you swear to be the antidote,
carry the cure within your clear glass bottle
As if to say that I'll want you slightly
more if I drink in what you pour before me
and it won't matter that I can't move
because you'll be there to place me
exactly the way you want me

See, late at night when I am finally alone
I ache all over—craving to be touched
betrayed each night by a body longing
for a simple act that
my brain will never allow me to enjoy

When Mom asks why I spend so much
time alone—I fear she still thinks
I am somehow allergic to love, as if
my body will become anaphylactic when touched
and I fear she might be right

What Mom doesn't know about is
the movie I play on repeat in the dark
in my bed: his face—always his blue eyes
the time he held my hand in his
fingers three inches longer than mine

Those very same fingers pressed

into my arms just above my elbows
to keep me from slipping away
in a strange bed, and I was too loud
Why am I always too loud?

It was like he knew he was wrong
but I wasn't strong enough to push him away
so as long as I remained quiet
I guess he sort of figured
that everything would work out okay—maybe

See, Mom, for me sex is a cancer
and I am never in remission long enough
to find a boy who might perhaps
want to stick around and see
if I'll ever be healed from my disease

I Stay Quiet

It is November, and
crisp breath, forms in the air
envelops my body in a sheath
of sticky, clammy, sick nervousness
at what is about to happen

He parks his Jeep near trees
I keep my mouth closed;
I stay quiet,
but my entire body reacts palpably
to the smell of pheromones
dense, and sticking inside the windshield

Bile rises in my chest
melts the protective layer
of my esophagus –
like a blowtorch put to a snowbank
scorches clear to the bone—
the skeletal scaffolding of the neck

I can't escape,
but, where would I go?
It is November, and dark;
a moon shows a fraction
of a hole to another dimension
where safety still exists.

In the vast treed land where,
I stay quiet—
the engine is killed,
I'm afraid if I

make the wrong move
I will be too
so, I am still.

Yet, my brain triggers alarms
scarlet halo illuminates the night,
my eyes and ears discern
danger
but, I can't
work out an escape
Hands tied behind my back,
And I'm blindfolded as if somehow
I'll forget what his face looks like
I am pushed down, first on my knees
where my mouth is filled
so I can't speak—

even if I could, no good would come
from my pleas for freedom.
Tears are meaningless
it is November, and frost
spreads up the windows
I stay quiet,
overcome by the stench
of sweat formed from fear
and naked body parts

I lie on my stomach
hips hitting the rough,
uneven, underside of seats
where slimy hands pull at my hair
direct a lifeless embodiment
where to go and how to get there.
I bite my lip, removing skin
blood salty like the tears
nobody sees,

taste sweet in comparison
to the sour that lingers
from the vulture behind

My body bruised
I am told exactly what to do
I stay quiet—
and cold in November
shiver from the sweat of another
smeared over my skin and
stealing what little heat I have left.

When it was over—finally over
hours, which felt like days,
have passed
stained milky white skin
red—
a scarlet letter I must wear
upon my breast—always

and no matter how hard I try
it will never go away
So, I stay quiet
become decay
hope to hide,
this disgrace

Who will listen when
I claim I just wanted to go
to the movies that night
in November, air crisp
a nice horror feature, to escape,
not to become part
of a horror I'd never escape

I'll take him and that night
with me everywhere now
for the rest of my life
when he put his hand on my thigh
and rubbed the inside
saying there was no time for a movie
Instead, he controlled me
late into the night.

It took me twenty-two years
to understand that any form
of non-consensual sex is rape
I thought it was my fault
when I didn't—couldn't fight back

Now, because of fear
there is no fight left in me
the memory of the Jeep's windows
rolled tight is a memory
I can never escape

I've become a blank canvas painted
forever in blood
the perfect portrait
of what it means for me to be a woman

I Have No Voice

and by voice I do not mean my ability
  to physically speak, I mean my ability
            to be heard. Sometimes I find myself
  lost in the repetition of exactly what I just said
  some close variation
            some warped variation
                        exactly—

I want to do more
            than simply exist. I want to thrive in a world
            where no means *no*
            where I do not have to fear for the betrayal of my
            body
            because it viciously craves touch—
            touch of man, that very touch that caused me
            to hate the fact that I am female, that I even exist
            at all.
            I wish I had known before
            twenty-two when I figured out that any form of
            nonconsensual sex
            was a form of physical abuse, that even though I
            finally said yes
            because no didn't mean *no* after all
            because I just wanted silence
            because your fingers became lighters scorching
            my inner thighs
            thinking I would change my mind.
            I wish you knew how it felt to cry yourself to
            sleep at night
            because your body quivers
            hungers to be touched, yet recoils the second it is.

I want to own my face,
        a sense of identity and belonging
        stripped from me at the age of six
        when in school my teachers told me
        I could never become a writer;
        the one thing that ironically
        ended up saving my life.

I guess I'm lucky that I don't recognize my own reflection
        in the mirror; there is no ownership there.
        I guess I am lucky because I can dress her up
        any way I please, like a Barbie I used to own,
        yet I do not own this one—
        almost as if she is borrowed
        from where I cannot be sure, where she'll be
        returned,
        or when is also unclear.

I guess I'm lucky because I get to wake up a blank slate
        each morning, attempt to create a persona
        I imagine whose body is not in constant agony
        from night terrors
        in which she cannot wake, whose body is a
        temple—
        not an item to be picked out by men for their
        amusement.

Most nights I do not sleep,
        terrified of what I see when I close my eyes,
        of where my brain goes when it is entirely at ease
        to be free after jumping over the walls
        I laid brick by brick, day after day in my mind
        in hopes to forget the fact that I wake
        up each morning nothing more than a stranger
        inhabiting this representation of a human.

I am completely invisible.
>By this I mean quiet, reserved, yet inside I am
>screaming
>a noise nearly inaudible to me. I am clawing just
>beneath
>the surface, where I am dying—
>to be seen by you. I just want you to love me,
>I want you to care, like I imagine a mother would
>for her beautiful daughter she was proud of—
>not that my mother never loved me;
>I know she did, yet somehow, I shut it out.

I know that you loved me so much,
>yet I walk around always with an empty void
>inside, as if I am somehow less of a girl,
>less of your daughter because of what men did to
>me.
>I know you still love me,
>but I can't help but wonder sometimes,
>if you would still love me knowing how broken
>I am inside, and how horrifically I crave
>the very thing that broke me in the first place.
> I know you still love me, so why is it not
>enough?
I wish I could love me.
>I wish I could live
>in a world where no means no.
>I wish I recognized the reflection,
>a shadow of a human staring
>back at me every morning.

Can you hear me now?

How to Measure Time

I.

I measure my existence in cigarettes
the tangible cylinder between fingers
that are a constant reminder of
the fact that I could only ever stretch
one octave and three keys in my pianist days
and friends who never played a day
could stretch two full octaves

What's My Age Again plays on my iPhone
becomes a portal to New Year's Eve
when I was sixteen years old and
couldn't wait to be twenty-three
There was a boy—
my sister's friend from high school
he was nineteen and
smoking a cigarette on the porch

I had just started that year
he asked me my age outside
I grabbed the cigarette, dangling
from my lips as I spoke
as if I were an adult in that moment
still very much sixteen
however old you want me to be

When he kissed me—like an adult
My first real kiss
something involving his tongue
I was suddenly drowning

in the tsunami I created
by longing to be twenty-three

His fingers were white caps
pinning me to the wall when
he tried to tear my shirt off
saying that I had been a tease
all night and I better give
him what he deserved

A single song lasted a lifetime
of seconds and missed chances
to get away—if only
I had been larger, or stronger
Then it ended and there was a drought
in the middle of the storm
releasing me, lightheaded and salty
to return to the party
officially entered into adulthood and how it felt—
the weight of what it meant to be a woman

II.

Time is death and those sweet
few seconds in between, when
you feel like infinity and forget to
think of the future because nothing
more matters than that moment

Like when I was eighteen and
he had no ring, but proposed anyways
and it was as if all the air in the world
had been removed and I became trapped
inside a vacuum of nothing but dust
and stale remnants of what

people never wanted—

He is the part I never wanted
tells me he has nothing else
to live for and one day he will
just drive into oncoming traffic
terrified, I tell no one

Bullet speed cannot be explained
until the day the phone call comes
from an old friend, so hysterical
I can't tell if she is laughing or crying
saying that his car swerved into
a mother and child, unharmed and
the world is somehow virtual and
nonexistent like it's constructed
from pixels which have now separated
creating an oblivion for him to remain in
Now every moment is spent wondering
about parallel universes where he must
still exist, some plain between
life and death that I must be able to access
even just a single moment to caress
the crooked frame of his once broken jaw
allow fingers to be scratched on
the pins and needles of his ginger stubble
but no matter how hard I try
there is always that divide—
fourth wall keeping me from him

So, I write non-fiction, poetry, broken lines,
anything to get him off my mind
title it It's Not Sexy When
a Man Says He Would Die for You
and it got published, but the void
of missed opportunities, unspoken words

bury themselves under my skin
keep me away from his grave
forever unable to say goodbye

III.

When a homeless man calls us—
my roommate and I, beautiful
I smile
longboard is distorted with the image of
a woman's face smeared on the bottom
some sadistic cross between a skull
and a clown that can stare directly
into my soul as if it knows my every secret
even I was unaware I possessed
some far-off glimpses of seconds from days
when I was four that were blocked off
for some reason unbeknownst to me

My roommate threatens to kill him
I assume it to be nothing more than
the fact that she is drunk—we are drunk
So, I throw myself between the two scrappers
as if I am somehow able to fill the gap
in my mind the face on the longboard knows about
that I somehow do not
and slip my tongue into the mouth of a stranger
breaking the screaming to fractals
of soundwaves on mute dissolving into the air
never to be heard again

Two fingers brush—lightly against dry lips
and I instruct him to go, just go
a moment just long enough for him to skate away
and for me to save a life

IV.

Time is always moving—reminding me just how
many moments are beyond my control
places and people I will never get back
memories become scar tissue on my brain
so, I can forget the pain this life has caused me

Always forward, never back
to relive what slipped through
the strainers
of my fingers
each moment a grain of sand
I have no real claim to
each moment borrowed from some promise
of an alternate reality of a better tomorrow
and somehow, all I can say is—
I ain't dead yet
so, I try and enjoy what little I have
before it dissipates like the rest

In Conversation with Today

Where do I belong?
I feel as if my body has become one
with the waves of the gleaming ocean bed
beyond the mountain tops of the island.
I watched as the sun melted into
the sapphire confines of the sky,
resting momentarily in the still
silence of the foreboding eve.
How I wish I could crawl into
bed with the sun, curl up in the melancholy song
of the wind and sleep for just a little while—weightless
and content, nonexistent to the moments passing
me by as I close my eyes. Just for a little while,
I wish the burdens that hold me hostage inside
my mind would subside, so the exhaustion
inhabiting my body would flit away
on a gust of wind and I could feel
weightless as a poem on a single piece
of paper forgotten in the street.

Heteronormative Monogamy

The penis goes into the vagina and
that's how you make a baby,
when you are married
mom told me when I was four
meaning mechanically babies came
from heteronormative monogamy
So, I was definitely blindsided at sixteen
when the first boy put his hands on me
and explained that it would be fun.
Mom knows best and she never
once mentioned fun
in fact, nothing much else was mentioned
in our home growing up

When she walks into the room,
a chalice of dance moves and smiles
hugging every person within a mile
I hear mom in the back of my head
the penis goes into the vagina
as if somehow, I am found guilty
of a crime that I have yet to commit
not that I've ever fantasized about
a woman or her body parts
because mechanically we don't fit

She looks in my direction
I look down—the penis goes into the vagina
and sometimes into my mouth
which mom also happened to leave out.
My lungs now comprised

of a year's worth of cigarette smoke
and my breath is lost somewhere in the haze
a feeling a man is supposed to provide—usually
before we are alone and I realize
he has been a trophy hunter the entire time
and my body is the prize
for his mantle display and
I am nothing more

Her lips are berry
voice sweet like the smoothie
I will go home the next morning
to drink away the hangover
of beer and confusion because
the penis goes into the vagina
and a penis is definitely something
she does not possess

The room is spinning and
I've had too much to drink—again
and the penis goes into the vagina
because it happens to fit and
my lower body screams and
that's how you make a baby
that's how it goes
but I'm not married
and the baby dies in the bathroom
in a coffee shop two months later

and I am left to mourn something
I never wanted in the first place
I make a cross marking
an empty plot of land in the forest
for a grave that I'll never visit because
how do I visit a grave

empty and hollow as the body
that expelled life in the first place?

See, I know coping methods
I know what it feels like
to curl into a ball in the darkness
in attempt to squeeze the void out of me
to be so high that my body spasms
as if each muscle hiccups simultaneously
sideways and is somehow unable to release

I've tried to cut off my own arm
in a hysterical stupor believing
that if I can't write the story
the story will die with me in a ball
in the corner of the room
filth covered and forgotten
I've woken up mornings
after murderous nights unsure
if I was covered in my own blood
or the blood of a stranger
perhaps a man who tried to tell me
the penis goes into the vagina
and I finally found the strength
to fight back against the phrase
I was raised to believe true

I imagine the shock of her lips
pressed against mine when
she is out of the room
flesh raises as if all the heat
in the world has been removed and
I wonder if my body craves
something it was never taught
that it could have

Or perhaps it is
a mere reaction to the fear
I feel from the very idea that
a man could do such damage and
I will never be bold enough
to toy with the emotions of another
because of the disease I inherited
from the knowledge that
the penis goes into the vagina

Then I grew up—moved on, travelled and
the thing with being a traveler
is that the chances of meeting her
again, are unlikely and
if it's really meant to be
she might find her way back to me
but probably not because
people aren't property
they can't be owned
and just because
the penis fits into the vagina
doesn't mean it belongs there

To My Father (A Didactic)

You sat with me on the living room stairs / buried my hand deep within Yours / You told me then, it was just a dream / and not to be afraid of the demons—who lurk like parasites / waiting in the dark for moments when we are alone / to invade / the brain / a fragile place / where things don't always make sense / You held me as if I was You— / an appendage / of a part of You / You wished never existed, yet couldn't let go / no matter how hard You tried / in that moment I was no longer alone / because I was Yours / every fucked up / heavily medicated / nearly / but never forgotten thought in Your brain / and had no reason to feel ashamed.

You always supported me / at times it seemed / You were the only one who backed up my dreams / of becoming a writer— / a poet / which I kept deep inside of me the way You kept the art deep inside of You / because You had a family to feed / but see, being a father, for me / meant more than the amount of money / You put down on the table each week / while You lived a life of misery / it was those moments / at night / when I was scared I wouldn't survive / and You showed me how with time / the demons would have less control of my mind / and I thought it was true.

Only, now / You lay dying in a hospital bed / and I'm not sure / if You ever believed / a word You said / to me / when I was so small and confused / as to why the world didn't make sense / You see, for me / time is like the ocean I moved to five years ago / to escape from the enemy trying to kill me / inherited from the blood / of You / still very much alive / existing within my veins / that 50% / of

genetic makeup / the most consistent thing / You have ever
given me, but / time ebbs, and it flows / it lulls, and it
goes—until eventually it's gone / and You don't get it back
/ if there's one thing life has taught me / it's how damn
beautiful things can be / when you take the time to live
consciously / instead of worrying about the demons / who
play hide and seek in the dark of Your mind / wondering if
they'll ever find where You hide.

I can't be with You as You die / I won't watch the life drain
from Your eyes / instead / I'll walk along the ocean's edge /
when it's dark, at eleven, or twelve / close my eyes / and
send out a message of love / in hopes that You feel me /
right there beside You holding Your hand / in mine while
You sleep / whisper in Your ear that it's just a dream / and
not be afraid of the demons who prey on Your mind while
You sleep / because You taught me it's okay / to be afraid /
because I had You / so, now, You have me / don't be afraid
/ because I won't bring flowers to Your grave / You are not
dead to me / You are every fucked up / confusing /
wonderful gene in my body / forcing me to find the will to
live / each day / even though I'm afraid / so, please / let me
repay the favor / because right now that's all I can give.

Confessions of an Addict: Sixteen Months Minus One Week Clean

I am a child of sin
        I turned my back on God at the alter
before I made it through my first communion
born from sin and constantly revisiting the shrine
in my mind from which I was resurrected
bathing over and over again in blood of the antichrist
himself
in an eternal hell that I've created where I walk alone

Which:
        by definition is the isolation from others
abandoned, deserted, and detached,
yet somehow never lonely
because I've grown accustomed to the lifestyle
that comes as a result of the demonic being
clinching the appendages of my form
claws tempered ablaze with the hours of wasted days
hook under the meaty flesh of this body—a sacrificial
monument
cauterizing the tissue before I have a chance to bleed
spawning scars which overlay rotten skin
the covering of an old directionless excuse of human

Now, where I come from
        people don't really understand
how it feels to have everything dropped at my feet

and to be willing to set fire to the bounty for no reason
other than to dance in the light of the beautiful flames
and for that momentary high from the fumes
of watching my every wish melt before my eyes,
yet too entranced to do a damn thing about it
so, I bask in the glory of such a mad possession of
sadness—

Once labelled an addict,
            the name follows in the shadows
for as long as I walk this earth—reaching towards the core
of my existence with its wispy finger-like projections
as the word itself, addict, and each
phlegm-casted daunting syllable lingers
the air in the room becomes stale with broken promises
and disappointed hopes for the sort of life that could have
been
before such a tantalizing name took hold of my hand
and lead me astray from the light at such a young age
teaching me to love the cold bitter darkness—
a place where nobody would dare come seek
the game from then on became just hide

Hide from the light and I'll be safe
            nobody will be brave enough to
put their own life at risk to pluck me
bring me back in their hand like a flower
and keep me on display in a vase
white and pure as the flower of death itself

The same lily that will be present at a wedding—
            my wedding
at a blossoming garden in April
that I didn't think I'd live long enough to see

the same wedding, I close my eyes to attend
at night when I can pretend that I wasn't exiled to live a life
of solitude in this purgatory
where I shall reside an entire lifetime
until my body will wither in the heat and I'll lay down to
die

See, now I live on borrowed time
          a second chance always comes
with the price of having to stare death in the face
haunted with disgust at the very idea that there was a time
where I would lay life itself on the line
just to have one more line
existing momentarily between the seconds of time
only living long enough to get from high to high,
but now, on borrowed time I have to figure out how
to live a life without getting high—remind myself
every single day

to stay clean,

          no matter how hard

                    that may seem

A Cigar is Never Just a Cigar

I dated a boy once for a short period
who smoked a cigar
the night we first fucked—
before we were a thing
he only smoked it because
I was smoking
said he had been saving it
for a special occasion
that cigar was the catalyst
for his smoking addiction
which he later blamed on me

We watched a movie once
About the sex trade
I left ten minutes in
went to bed disgusted
later he crawled on top of me
breath sticky and predatory
there was something about
those movies that made him so horny
we had sex until I cried—
kicked him out and smoked

We broke up in July that year
two days before his birthday
over the phone—he smoked a cigar
claimed it was my fault
he was still smoking

My Demise

The bombs first fell 9 days ago. I did not see them,
but I cried.
There was rain all week. I don't like the rain.
I fell asleep last month. I did not see them,
but they broke my face. They scraped my insides,
Hollowed out my head.
There was a 3% chance I would end up dead.
But I didn't die. Instead, I survived.
In a world where I'm not sure that I want to be alive.
I heard your strings ring out in the night.
Reminded me of a place where I wanted to be high.
Now I'm not sure if I still want to be high,
Or if I simply want to die.
Being stuck in a world of lies.
In a body that I don't recognize.
No soul to identify. I feel hollow and empty.
Alone in a room. Inside of my head.
Which they scraped out. A reflection I don't recognize.
Stuck with the demons inside I thought they would take.
But they only took flesh. That was my mistake.
I don't want to die, I don't think.
I just don't want to keep living.
Not in a world so full of hate.
Inside a body that feels no pain,
Yet a mind that cries at every line.
And I'm still here.
I didn't die. I don't want to die.
I just don't want to be alive.

The Aftermath of Abuse

You tell me you love me and my first
instinct is someday you won't and

that fucking terrifies me to be open and
vulnerable enough to maybe for a little while

trust the words that come from your mouth

And before I know it, I'm pounding
against the walls of my brain which are pounding
against the walls of your apartment
a chain of dolls unfolding
body dismorphing time distorting

and again, I'm spiraling
lower and lower
to the darkness that tells me
I don't deserve to be with somebody like you
where I dwell on every imperfection
trying not to believe the lies
that Facebook sells me
in the ads that tell me about fattening recipes,
workout methods and clothes I can never afford

to fit in at the job I got where I am still fucking bored
but don't make enough money
for my room and board and I'm
constantly bombarded with things
I'll never be able to afford
So, I spend each shift pretending
that I live a life where I can own that shit

and that I can deserve to be loved by a man
as beautiful as you
and stop worrying about the fact that we both have dreads
and what people must think of us when we walk
in the room
how our kind has begun to spread
but we stick together as if bound
together by locks of hair
unable to be ripped apart

I want to tell you that I love you
to just say the words out loud
but my tongue catches the L
as the bile rides the reflex wave of my esophagus channel
and I gag play it off as a stumble
or a half-asleep mumble
worried about the permanence of the spoken word

and let me just say,
I know all about the spoken word because
I'm a performance artist
who teaches youth of the power
of speech and finding their voice
yet I gasp like attacked each time
I try to pry my lips apart
as if you would dissipate
the moment, I spoke the four-letter word

and I think about fairy tales and
a happily ever after that will never
truly exist on this plane
and I feel shame for the mascara
burning my eyes in the bathtub
my first night alone without you
and all the time I've wasted being glued to your side
but what else could I do

when I met a man who didn't make my skin feel like fire
when he rubbed me in
all the previously wrong places made right

but, see, I'll never truly be right
in the head constantly waiting for the end
like our first fight that happened in bed
because of miscommunication
because I thought men only want women for
their bodies so I gave it to you and
you tossed it aside
because, see, you saw more of me
than a dismorphed body could ever really be
but how can I trust that,
when I can't even find the strength yet
to look in the mirror and decide for myself
that I am more than a body
that I still don't recognize, which makes
no fucking sense
because how can I inhabit a body
that I know so little about
and how can I trust that you love me
when I don't even understand who I am

Yet, to my surprise, you are gentle and kind
and don't leave behind bruises on my body
or pain in places that make me
feel used like a punching bag
taped back together to appear less abused
to the public when they pass by
during their daily routine
and my family tells me I appear
happier than I have in the last five years
as if I would understand
the glow left behind like a shadow
from a halo named happiness looming

around my head like a crown
I was born into my spot on the throne
but being conditioned my entire life
to end up at a destination
like the dog Pavlov trained to salivate
he doesn't choose to understand
why he does this at every bell
I just learned that we are supposed to be happy
and smile and feel this bubble inside when in love
but I can't dissect how looks on the outside
I don't understand why
but I do remember when I called my mom and said,
I thought I had stomach cancer
because my organs were moving
and nothing seemed in line anymore
I couldn't sleep and my heart was beating
irregularly my stomach continuously twitched
I guess those are what the cliches call "butterflies"
which is a load of shit if you ask me
because why should I feel like I'm dying
when I feel happiness in its purest form for the first time
and why should I be self-conscious enough to want to hide

yet when I'm with you I don't feel shame,
nor do I want to run and hide
because you said burning man rules apply to
everything in life:

1. Consent
2. Fun
3. Safety

As if somehow,
I have a claim to my body for the
first time in over two decades
only you are serious

and I'm not sure what to make of that
to own the bag of bones I've been dragging along
all this time a temporary lease waiting to be revoked
by the next man who takes a piece through conquest
and one less part of me remains
in the bag that I drag along
So, tell me, do I open the bag
and put back piece by piece what's left
and how would that work?
The neck bones connected to the shoulder bone,
the shoulder bones connected to is it chest bone,
collar bone, connected to the rib bone?
Missing bones, bones cracked under the pressure
of silencing my screams
for so many years when they touched me

and now I want to scream
louder than I've ever screamed before
that I love your body and mind
the way you watch informational
YouTube videos to fall asleep to
and the fact that you built me a bed
so I could stay over because
you were inhabiting your living room couch
the way your breath feels on my neck
when you sleep and the feel of your eyelashes
blink against my back while you dream and
when your roll over still asleep pull me in close
and kiss my cheek
and my forehead when we're awake and I am safe
but nothing more than a whisper can escape
and I fear you feel I don't love you
the way you say you love me in so many ways
and that even though you say you won't leave
one day you will grow tired of my flesh-eating
body-dismorphing disease because

you won't believe that I love you
and you will forget how to love
an old bag with missing bones
that is supposed to represent a human I suppose
but I wouldn't really know
and you say for now one day at a time
my request of course
but how much time must pass
before I feel whole
and can learn to trust you
with my entire soul,

But now, somehow, with you
every muscle begins to twitch
and my breath again is trapped
I scream internally which equates to
nothing more than a whimper
and I crash exhausted in a heap as if
you have removed each
remaining bone with your teeth
and I wouldn't mind it
if you owned what was left,
but then you place them back
piece by piece exactly where they came from
because I am not property and cannot be owned
but I still don't know what
to do with this old bag of bones

You tell me you love me
and my first instinct is someday you won't
and that fucking terrifies me
to be open and vulnerable enough to maybe
for a little while trust the words that come
from your mouth and to trust somewhere from within
myself to say those three little words out loud
I love you.

In Conversation with Myself — III

What if I were to end by saying I had fallen in love
With the image sprawled before my mind
if the concept that life takes on many forms
perspective varies through the lens of each observer
malleable and precious

Perhaps if I were to tell you that time is measured
by each exhale and begins again on the inhale
that each one of us has the power between the two
to choose life
rebirth
new growth
or stagnance encompassed by the conscious
choice to not inhale again
you would comprehend

Suppose I told you that you had the power
all the power to shift perspectives
would you be willing to change the outcome?

www.ingramcontent.com/pod-product-compliance
Lightning Source LLC
LaVergne TN
LVHW050932200726
843508LV00011B/2325